HEAvY LEAD
BIRDSONG

poems by Ryler Dustin

1

Heavy Lead Birdsong

Ryler Dustin

Write Bloody Publishing ©2008

1st printing.

Printed in NASHVILLE TN USA

Cover Designed by Brandon Lyon, Illustration by Scott Winters

Interior Layout by Lea C. Deschenes

Edited by Derrick Brown, Saadia Byram and Michael Sarnowski

Illustrations

Contact these contributing artists for quality work:

Chelsea Thoumsin: chelsea.thoumsin@gmail.com

Tiara Anderson: taira.L.a@gmail.com

Scott Winters: scottywinters@gmail.com

WRITEBLOODY
QUALITY AMERICAN BOOKS AND PRINTING

Heavy Lead Birdsong

Dedication

For Bob, for Graham, for Jessica, for Bellingham.

For my friends there, the best I've ever had.

For Denise.

For Jason.

For Karen, with deep gratitude.

For Aliesha, who I'm never alone with.

For Jack Gilbert, Li-Young Lee, James Tate, Sharon Olds, Ralph Waldo Emerson, Carl Sagan.

For Robert Penn Warren's "Masts at Dawn."

For the poets who tithe with sleep.

Foreword

The other day I saw an article on the National Public Radio website about a violinist named Julia Fischer. There was a live recording of her playing Bach. About halfway through one of the songs, it struck me: she wasn't putting her energies into playing, she was putting them into listening. She was listening harder than everyone else in that whole silent auditorium – she was hearing something the rest of us couldn't hear – maybe that perfect rendition of Chaconne, that one that is impossible to achieve, that exists only in the mathematical perfections of the imagination. Maybe something more like rainwater. Maybe her childhood, maybe all of our childhoods.

She was acting as an intercessor.

I started writing because I thought it might preserve my name, and all the things attached to it – might prevent the past from swallowing up so much that has happened to me. Many poems in this collection, the ones I wrote earliest, come from that place of desperation; many were written afterward from a place of mourning, as I learned that nobody's name or history lasts forever. But the better I became at listening, the more I began to hear something beyond my own name: another name, maybe, or a current, a song, something worth study.

One of my favorite poets, Li-Young Lee, said in an interview that he thinks religion is "fossilized poetry." That strikes me as true, and I like how it implies that perfection and "completeness" are unnecessary in a poem; that the prayer of poetry is fluid, still alive and moving. It makes me feel better about releasing such a substantial collection containing so much old work. Though I have taken care to create continuity in Heavy Lead Birdsong, it is still a moving creature, created from all the styles and ideas I've explored in the past four years. These poems, like their author, are works in progress, the way all poems remain as long as they are alive. I can only hope that a poem, like any other prayer, does not have to be perfect in order to be worthy.

— Ryler Dustin

Medieval stonemasons
carved swallows on the walls
to symbolize escape…

the masons' champion
gone up the rays of light
to plead their case to angels

— **Malcolm Kenyon**

BOOK ONE

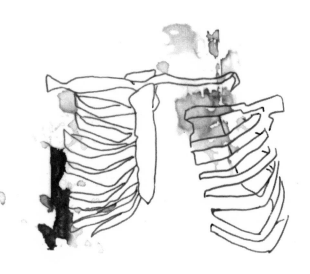

Seven Codas

Some of us will die from hearing too many cars
pass the road near our homes.
Or the sidewalk trees rustle too many times.

Our brain keeps track of these things, like an abacus,
and when the last bead is moved
a web of nervefire rockets off transmitters
that tell our body, *Rest, stop, it's alright,*
I've seen enough, I'm full now.

Some of us will die from sketching wet red self portraits
down our forearms, from wanting to escape life so badly
that we do.

Some of us will die from wonder.
Some of us think too much about Phineas Gage,
about which part of us is us
and what, if anything, will remain of it.
We are consumed finally by the overwhelming,
expanding width of the universe.

Some of us will die kissed by tubes on hospital beds
being fed intravenous math that adjusts our consciousness,
our level of pain versus disorientation.
We'll have to struggle harder than we've ever struggled for anything
to look out the window between breaths of saline solution

and thought-bending morphine

to realize

that's

rain

outside.

Some of us, like my mother,

will break the windows of our nursing homes

and run into the forest to starve like rebels and heroes.

Some of us will die holding a comrade's head

in the ash of a battlefield,

thinking in the very end about everything

except killing.

Some of us will die in our sleep.

Some sleepyellers like me will jab a sword

down the throat of a familiar bad dream

and be tangled up in the deaththroes of its tentacles,

uprooting our blankets in private nighttime spasms,

dragging our fears with us into black, secret glory,

wrestling with the bird skeleton of our boyhood nightmares

over the last sunset hill,

down the cliff of ending,

like Sherlock and Moriarty

into the freedom of dark.

That is how I have believed I would die

since I was young.

But sometimes,

wonder

seems just as likely.

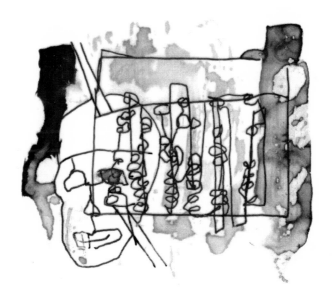

The Country of Her Lungs

Every day, my mom watches *Day Star*.
The Billy Graham reruns in faded blue light
make me feel like I'm underwater.

Her house is a perpetual baptism.

Today, the TV is offering a book called
God's Answers to our Deep Hurts.

Outside, for free, the snow is falling.

My mom is a country with lots of rivers
and bridges falling into them.

She is the only person I love so intensely
it feels like a sickness, like fear.

I can't wait for her senility to kick in.

Then we'll be able to talk in poetry
and finally agree about the shape Christ's wind
should take in our lungs.

Allie

Baby girl,
you're big.

Big like all those times
you balled your fists
and told some boy *no*.

Big like the teethwide smile
that split your happy ten year old cheeks
when I bought you that plastic ruby
in a checkout line
with my own money.

Big like your crying
that filled our empty house
after Dad got married
without telling us.

You're big like that propeller toy
I got tangled in your hair
when you were three,
big like my fingers
trying to work a splinter
out of your skin,
big like that fifth grader
I beat into the bushes with his bicycle

after he touched you.

Baby girl, you're big
like our five foot mother.

Big like the cars
that roared past our blue house
when you were four and I was six,
big like the job of keeping an eye on you
while we played,
big like the thrashing in my ribcage
after I let you get too close to the end
of the driveway.

Big like my sleepyelling
when it cracks through our sleeping house,
big like the thick bright tire-mounted bullets
in my recurring dream,
big like my six year old hand
grabbing your tiny shoulder
to spin you back
from the noise of the street.

Baby girl,
you're big.

You always have been.

But old instincts die hard

and I still remember when you needed

a big brother

while I sleep.

Heavy Lead Birdsong

Dear reader, we are the same, our eyes sit

like heavy windows in black stone

like widows sewing by lamplight

in houses that are too small

to hold their heavy lead birdsongs.

Cosmology

One evening, God grew restless

when we could not satisfy his loneliness

and took a horse and carriage to a city

to apprentice in a trade he had never heard of.

Glassblowing, maybe.

He is blowing glass in a red-windowed shop

veiled by snow. His face is lined

and he has long, tanned limbs.

He sends us letters from time to time,

suggesting we read children's books

inappropriate for our age.

Does not bother to send us a photo.

But we picture him in his shop, puffing and spinning,

trying to uncurl peace

from his own mathematical dedication.

Years pass. We stop hoping he will return.

In our beds at night, we still think of him.

We stand outside his shop in our dreams,

watching his fire balm the windows in gold.

Glass fills with his breath, burns and slouches

at the end of his tongs.

We strain our sight through the snow

to watch his smoky forehead,

his frowning face,

his long back bending like calligraphy,

as elegant, as pure.

Bellingham Public Library

When I read books in my bedroom,

the voices in those pages make the sound of running water.

I fall asleep with rivers of ink on my chest.

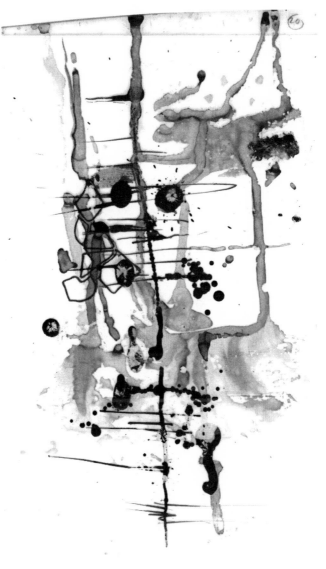

Blackbirds

If I ever decided to believe in angels,
I'd believe in street wanderers
watching us from alleyways
and the sides of greasy dumpsters,
hanging on gutters,
drinking out of paper bags from rooftops,
muttering in the shadows about human struggles,
unanswered prayers, the demons snickering
between our shoulder blades.

They'd communicate with each other
through the curling graffiti
that most of us assume is the work of some gang
but none of us can really understand.

Warnings like, *Look out for Ryler.*
I overheard that kid talking to himself
for the first time in eight years
about how suicide is starting to sound
like another word for clean.

Or, *Tina's picked up her crack habit again.*
Izrafel and I saw her light up last night
by the warehouse two blocks west.
Be ready for damage control.
She's gonna cause trouble for people,

gonna start stealing stuff they aren't ever
gonna get back –
and this time we're not just talking about
her husband's wristwatch.

They'd cover their faces
with knobby, frostbitten fingers
every time we'd stumble past at midnight
hoping we'd be sly enough
to hook someone's heart at the bar.
They'd grin rotting teeth
and suck their stogies with joy
whenever someone in dreadlocks stops
to help a businessman pick up the papers
that have scattered from his briefcase.

If I believed in angels,
they wouldn't have white robes
that burnt our eyes like salt
or faces like Roman statues.

They'd be braver than that.

They'd be covert spies
deep in enemy territory.

They'd be hunted by things you and I can't see
except on bad acid trips.

They'd have their heads down, eyes smoldering,

sitting vigilant at closing time

in gasoline painted puddles, sucking rum,

like Vietnam rangers

unable to sleep

for more than forty seconds at a time

not just because they're keeping watch

but because they've seen humans do things

that only heaven could wash out of their dreams.

If they ever gave up

and went back.

If I believed in angels,

they'd be the ones

who wouldn't

go

back.

They wouldn't look like Filippo Lippi's choirboys

or six-winged Catholic seraphim,

wouldn't part the world's darkness around them

like Roman candles.

They'd be scared.

And strong.

They'd have broken bottles instead of flaming swords.

They'd be fighting with shadows like schizophrenics.

They'd be sending us desperate blessings

from barrel-fire séances.

They'd be whispering in low voices about

who's gonna win the war

like Jews

hiding in the shadows of Copenhagen.

They'd shudder from flashbacks

of something terrible they tried to stop

every time they saw a clothes hanger.

They'd be sending each other encoded

long distance

prayer lists

spray painted on locomotives.

They'd be leather skinned women

and stocking cap men,

and only a few of us would ever notice them:

their black-stained feathers

hidden down trench coats

or hooded sweatshirts,

their insomniac eyes

        scanning the streets,

their backs against the walls

of alleyways

slick

with names

   and rain.

The Clouds Over Georgia

1.

I took a nighttime plane out of Georgia two years ago,

left Maria crying in the airport with her mother,

whispering she was sorry. After all the antidepressants,

the thrashing, the pushing me against white walls

and pouring of candle wax onto herself and me holding her

back from the knives in the kitchen –

now there was only this soft light,

the hum of the turbines,

a Virginia Woolf book she'd given me.

I had expected blood to stain some of the pages

or to find broken fingernails buried near the spine

but there were only watermarks.

Around page fourteen, I remembered

that Virginia Woolf had walked into a stream.

I drifted between sleep and these thoughts,

dreaming of the stewardesses who rustled around

like wardens of time, collecting used cups,

snatching up discarded wrappers,

putting blankets on passengers, closing the books

left open on our drowsing chests,

pausing in front of windows

now and again

to make changes in the clouds.

2.

The clouds over Georgia are like Maria.

By evening they're very tired, worn out

from the afternoon cry, left thin and ravaged.

It's part of a cycle. The next day

they will swell again, collecting the water

that evaporates off ditches and streams, thickening

until they can't contain themselves any longer

and rain explodes across the hot streets.

But now it's dusk. They've cried themselves

into exhaustion.

Two weeks before the flight, I'd let out

my own little rainstorm in a gas station bathroom

after Maria had yelled at me

for losing her half-empty bottle of Aquafina.

3.

I had also been dreaming of my bookmark.

It was not the best picture of her,

or the one of her naked on my bed.

It was the photograph her mother had given me

from when Maria was eight years old,

perched on a big white rock

in jean shorts and a pink tank top,

smiling the way she always would:

crookedly, hugely, with her eyes.

Stirring awake, I realized that the Virginia Woolf book

had fallen to the empty seat beside me.

There was a rustle, something fast and almost soundless,

the blur of a uniform moving past,

and then the book was closed.

The bookmark was gone from sight.

There was only the cover now –

blue, old, slightly warped and stained

from water, or rain, or tears.

Bronze Birdsong

When they open my father's chest
on the autopsy table,

they'll find a small snow globe
like a pearl inside his heart. As they shake it,

flakes of shrapnel will fall
instead of snow across a jungle

where tiny men wade across a river,

fumbling with cigarettes,
tossing grenades into the bushes.

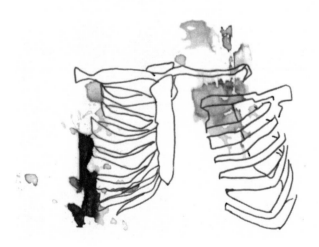

My Old Man

When you're young, love rests awkward
    against your stomach,
wears a red hat, has your left lung tied around its wrist
    like a blue balloon. But my love wheezes
        like an old man when it sleeps.

When it sleeps, I cannot sleep.
    When it's awake, I'm even worse for sleep.
    The old man keeps me up.
        He rocks in his old chair, cursing and asking someone
            to feed the cats.
    There are no cats in my chest.
    The old man is crazy.

I took away his typewriter because the keys
    kept me up all night.
But now he scratches poems on the inside of my tongue.
    I don't know how he gets up there.
    He writes poems to strangers
        just to fuck with me.
    He writes poems to big breasted women.
        He writes poems to the bodies of women
            and forgets to put the women in them.
        He writes poems to men with business suits on
            who have forgotten their stories
                aren't boring,

to old ladies crossing the street

and lovers crossing themselves

against what their skin wants to do,

to the ones who rush into love too early,

knowing it will not last,

praying Lord, please keep me strong

and lonely through all of this

so it does not hurt when I rip pleasure

back out of my body.

My old man laughs like a grandmother with a shotgun

blowing my poems out of the sky –

Not good enough! Not good enough!

He's more like a leprechaun than a cupid.

He falls in love with buildings.

He falls in love with what people leave behind them:

new hairpins and old architecture and apple cores.

He hoards apples in my chest

and now my chest is full of apples.

My chest is growing into a tree.

Trees are aching inside of it

like it's a too-small pot

and the old man is swinging from the branches, yelling

Give me back my typewriter,

you stupid fuck,

look what you are doing to yourself!

So I swallow harder

and type for the both of us: I type love poems to my mother that
say

     Thank you for the days
you smiled like a broken fountain
     and put my problems first.

     I type love poems to my sister that say
          When you have died I will go to your hospital bed
     and mark where heaven was planted.

     I type love poems to my father that say
This poem is clearly-phrased and technical.
It is not over-concerned with aesthetics.
This poem reads books like *The Seven Habits
of Highly Effective People*. It is like a raft from a desert island
or you when your father hit you so hard
you landed in Viet Nam.
It survives no matter what.
Hopelessness crosses this poem's mind
but not its heart – this poem hopes
with all its crossed heart for life.
This poem drinks principles, Father,
this poem coughs on itself, Father,
this poem coughs on itself because it is trying to be bigger
than the man who birthed it, but it is just these slung-up words,
just these makeshift words slung up in the mouths of strangers
     to prop them open and let the light out,
this poem is broken   on your knee, Father, take it up,

33

like a necklace, like a wire box, like a birdcage,

like something functional, like a sniper rifle,

like a call for backup, like divorce counseling,

like a repairable heart, and place it on your bookshelf

between *The Power of Now* and *How to Forgive your Abusive Parent*

or inside the cover of *How to Forgive Your Alcoholic Father*

On His Deathbed and then Raise your Children

the Way He Should Have, the way you did,

take this poem into your arms the way you did,

teach this poem to forgive itself

    so it will stop beating me up from the inside,

hold it softly in your hands like a brittle leaf,

like a sunset you could eat like an orange,

like the apples in our backyard,

like the trees in our backyard   you used to prune for us every summer,

like every summer igniting into autumn   in our chests,

in licks of red flame and copper wire   and piano notes

    I want to hang for you in the sky.

Baptism

The truth is, I looked at pornography

before I started to write tonight.

It wasn't that I wanted to look.

It was that I wanted not to want it anymore.

Sometimes I'm shocked by an emptiness and I stop.

But tonight the math of the body unfolded,

eyes like cities and hips that burned like fields of barley.

It began to rain outside, as if the women

had tipped the hand of God.

Outside, people were buying cigarettes, groceries,

shivering in a way angels cannot replicate.

We are never comfortable in our own skin

because it is utterly perfect. Young men

drunk on themselves, rushing past my street,

yell that they will never grow old.

The people we love have roadmaps to home

drawn in the folds of their skin

but so many of us search and search and never arrive

because searching is what we have done

for so long. There is a theorist who believes

language came to us as we hunted, that learning to read

the signs of our prey in the wilderness

filled us with symbols – hoof, hair, bent fern…

Something can mean without being. Something can imply.

A photograph can be like a woman. A woman

can hold a whole ocean inside of her. And men, too.

Some men with large noses and deep circles under their eyes
remind me of God, or of my own face,
which looks like His as he pauses, frowning,
lost in the forest.

Why We Do Not Go Out

for Karen

Every week, my girlfriend and I
say that we should go hiking.
But we never do.

Last week our excuse was the cold.
The week before, it was the rain.

Today our excuse was that we got stoned.
The sky was so heavy around her apartment
that a wilderness grew inside of us,
waterfalls like white wrists,
forests with high dark trees
where insects beat dusk into the air
like a child rinsing her paintbrush
in a glass of water.

We were cartographers lost
in the country of ourselves.

When I leaned close to her chest,
I could hear the grasshoppers crooning,
the birds committing their vespers,
the last drowsy bees hanging like music notes,
carrying pollen from flower
to flower.

BOOK TWO

By the River

Suppose we could iridesce,

like these, and lose ourselves
entirely in the universe...
        - Mark Doty, *A Display of Mackerel*

A man named Ronald died
without anyone to mourn him
and was featured in a documentary called
A Certain Kind of Death.
What I remember is how many photographs
glistened like fish in his bookcase.

A state employee with rubber gloves
held one up for the camera:
Ronald, nine years old,
hair swept under waves of sepia.

Who teased him when he was a kid?
Or was he the bully? How often
have we held our own histories in our hands,
wondering who lived that other life?

I sometimes imagine having this job,
removing the detritus of the forgotten dead.
Would it be the opposite of writing

or almost the same thing?

How it would hush my swollen ego

to plunge my hands into those abandoned bookcases,

to wrestle whole schools of slippery memories

to the surface, to hold them as the traffic

rushed down the street outside,

then put them in a box to be burned.

When the last person forgets this documentary

about the forgotten dead,

and the last person forgets this poem,

Ronald's soul will finally slip the rungs of his name.

He'll pass at last through the doors

of whatever kingdom or nothingness

waits for us, is our home.

Your Heart Was Once a Hill

A big hand chiseled wild horses from its side.

Now the horses fill you.

When the rain sweeps over your roof at night,

you hear them sweeping, too.

You are possessed by the strange, proud beauty

of your pulse.

Inside your body, it is always dusk

and Montana.

At night, when you wake up alone,

you're terrified that one of the horses is missing.

That one of them got away.

So you look for it, in your body

and in the bodies of others.

Somewhere there's a bent tree

on the prairie.

A horse stands beside it, its mane and tail

like Arabic.

As you move closer,

you can faintly see

small children dancing around a fire

in its chest.

The Gilded Afternoon

A swarm of golden locusts came to my town one day.
Their compact, glistening bodies dented the cars
until traffic stopped.

We watched from our porches and storefronts
as they dripped like sap from the telephone lines,
as the wind's blood turned to amber.

They chewed away the gravel in our driveways,
severing the bridge between where we were
and where we thought we were supposed to be,
afflicting us with childhood.

A man in the grocery store where I was working
stopped cussing at his nine year old son
and stood like Greek ruins, mesmerized.

In his eyes I could almost see the memory
of the hair of a woman who left him.

My mother was reading the Bible on her porch
when one of the locusts splashed into her coffee
like a fat coin trying to buy the dusk.
When she dropped her cup, the shattering porcelain
whispered back new scripture:
Maybe there can be such a thing

as a plague of beauty.

She thought somebody in Egypt
had built a monument to Christ
and the world was being rewarded
with strange reversals of the Seven Plagues,
that our firstborn sons would live forever.

But I was not praying to live forever,
only for the moment
as I fell to my knees outside the grocery store

thinking how the ambition-consumed lawyer women
that I used to fantasize about were now only
the second most beautiful things in my town.

How my ex-girlfriend, with her radiant face that carries autumn,
was now the third most beautiful thing in my town.

How even her new boyfriend
who is terribly silent and in an important band
must be stunned somewhere
watching this afternoon eclipse of the mundane,
these wings folding and unfolding
into a million secret handshakes to God per second,

this air alive with a funeral prayer
for our vanity.

The locusts have left, but I remember:

we've all been knocked down one notch on the scale

of most beautiful things to have existed,

and for one evening

in my town

we were unafraid to watch the sunset.

The Long Night

After Amy and I had left the first bar,

after we'd made friends with the Australian man

who paraded his accent for American girls,

after he was 86ed for getting into a fight

in the bathroom of *The Beaver*

while I was outside talking on the phone

to my girl who was visiting Maryland,

after I had ordered another pitcher of beer

and then, like an owner being courteous to a pet fish,

more beer to keep it company,

as Amy was losing to the boys at pool

but winning the boys over,

she snapped her fingers and said,

I have a friend you can stay with tonight

so you don't have to drive.

That's how I ended up at the house of her friend,

also named Amy, talking, still drunk,

trying not to accidentally imply

we should make out, which seems easy

but is sometimes oddly difficult

in situations like that.

She gave me her bed and took the couch,

and as I lay in the soft sheets,

I wondered if I should have refused the gesture,

if it were legal in terms

of my new but committed relationship

to sleep on my side, snuggled up

to Amy's friend Amy's pillow,

or if I ought to lie straight on my back

making sure not to smell anything.

The nightlight was bright enough

that I could make out the dresser,

cluttered with photographs of Amy and her friends,

perhaps some of them also named Amy,

and it struck me, looking at all those smiles,

that our lives are so ridiculously long,

that our biographies are like awkward plays

or poems that ramble on too much,

that the whole act of being young

is just trying to distract ourselves

from the knowledge that, by the end of this,

we will scarcely remember

how any of it

got started.

Cobalt Birdsong

When my ex-girlfriend dreams,

her apartment is smeared with the color of twilight.

She wakes up and has to replace her blue eye shadow.

I got her the letters of van Gogh for her birthday.

Sometimes I see her at the bar.

If her friends make her laugh hard enough,

the air above her boils,

singing like *Starry Night.*

Anatomy and Physiology

From the bottom of four chambers
and a sense of not owning anything,
this is a love poem.

From when I pressed my ear to your stomach and said,
Can you believe that right now
blood is lacing itself through all those cells?

How, near this curve, liquid is drained by the kidneys?
How, up here, breath dissolves into heat?

You were born with all the eggs you will ever produce
and they sit in the dark
turning while I listen.

But you pulled my hair to make me look up.
You wanted the usual clichés.

I love you because you are beautiful.
I love you because of the way you style your miracle hair
without ever wondering how it grows.

I love you because we are young
and youth is fashionable
and love, in some circles, is fashionable.

But listen.

From the bottom of four chambers

and a sense of owing you something,

this is a confession.

The whole time, I could think only

of the warm, steady humming of the miracle.

When I shut my eyes, I saw a red flower,

veins rising through tissue, bleeding a perfect dialect.

If it is any consolation, I've spent these last few nights awake

hunting by lamplight for the parts of love we weren't able to find.

I fall asleep beside *Gray's Anatomy*, college lab packets

with elegant diagrams, the words turning slowly on my tongue,

aorta, sartorius,

   clavicle, gracilis.

We'll Vanish Like Cities

I've come here
all wrapped in clothing
to keep me in
keep you out
but actually if you smile like that
and smooth back my hair
our clothes will vanish
like cities will vanish
like cars will rust
like fire hydrants wither
like moss roll itself
out over the pavement
and trees spring up
from all the cracks
and humanity sigh
into nothing
into wind
into desert sand
into ocean flotsam
into boiling stardust
and northern lights
into astral currents
into fuel
into ten minutes of sunlight
for some alien race

leaving you and me here
unguarded
hopeless
and forced by the loneliness
of being the only ones
not soaring around as ions
to make an awkward and beautiful love
that will shrink in your memory
this memory
of what we did
will catch a breeze
out your open window
with artificial potpourri

candle scent
and spent
ignited pheromones
and swell into the sky
and color the stars
in a way
that only
the great artists
could see

before they all turned
into moss food
and sun dust.

Then our scent
will vanish
the way great artists
vanish
the way great art
and small art
means in the end
just a single sheet
of common poetry
that gets crumpled up
and becomes ten minutes
of fire
        in some giant's hearth,
flaring and vanishing
the way we
will vanish
the way cities   will vanish
the way we   will vanish
the way you   will vanish
the way we   will   vanish
the way cities   will vanish
the way we
        were   something
the way you
        were   something
the way we   did   something
the way
    you

were beautiful

while

you burned.

The Sex That Could Have Been

A busted window with blood in the cracks. The same sweet
toothsucking pain that makes good poetry. Collar-upturned
nightwalks past neon lit smoke. Smiling from across a
sidewalk. Circles under your eyes. A raft burning at sea.
The smell of flannel and soap. A hot marble under your
tongue. Insects frozen in a winter pond. Fistheld firecrackers
bound in rice paper. Mutual fear of not getting to the bottom
of each other. Not sleepyelling anymore. Escaping language.
A nervous bird restrained gently. The sound of rain on a window.

Better than Being Alone in my Room

One night I was so lonely and bored that when Rachel called me up at nine to invite me to a party, I exploded in my shoes and landed in my car with it already in neutral and rolling out of the driveway.

When Rachel and Berkley and I got there and slammed out of the car, chagrin crept up my face like champagne bubbles, like the realization that Rachel's friend's party was actually being hosted at Rachel's aunt's friend's house, whose roommate was a heavyset thirty-something who interviewed me on the front porch about some eighties movie and I had to answer correctly or at least be attractive to get in. Fortunately, older ladies don't care about how skinny my arms are, so she let me pass as she gave cigarettes to a couple of young girls, silhouetted against the moths that ate up the porch light.

I saw the moths eating when my hand touched the doorknob, and I should have known that was bad prophecy, a metaphor for the upcoming. But my poet sense was overridden by my poet loneliness and besides, I was probably hoping my soul mate would be inside, throwing up and asking for someone to hold back her hair.

When Rachel and Berkley and I went in, everything melted into early teenage screams, like freshmen year of high school screams, with loud bubblegum hop pop soda spilling in Technicolor through the speakers of the Jessica Simpson boom box, some young girls dancing like new drunks and other young girls standing around like it was the five minute break between class periods.

There was only one other guy there, a boyfriend who couldn't have been older than sophomore year and I felt like a pedophile.

But then that eighties-movie-thirty-something-lady came in and started making me strange mixed drinks, and whispering to the girls about me, and keeping her black makeupped eyes all over me until that concerned I'd had about being a pedophile melted into a sick reversal.

Some friends of mine showed up and that helped to lessen the tension until they were caught smoking pot on the front porch, and hell exploded like a melon in a microwave, and everyone was yelling and upset and *why did anyone bring men to this party anyways?!* and the eighties-movie-thirty-something began stumbling around, drunkenly yelling about how we had to keep it down,

> stomp,
>> stomp,
> scReam,
>> stomp,

because her sons were sleeping upstairs, a five and a six year old.

I almost threw up my heart.

But instead I started talking, slurring apologies and no hard feelings and *Sure, I agree, men are stupid,* thinking *Please Ryler, hold it together, don't start crying, don't start thinking about the kids, just keep her talking at a relatively normal volume* until finally she went upstairs, after cursing out the male half of the species one last time, thank God softly, and saying I was welcome in her house anytime.

Things settled into a soft, dim silence. I put blankets on the girls who had passed out, then stretched out under the Christmas tree. I lay there waiting to get sober, watching the white, old-fashioned lights. It was long past the holiday season. I never learned why it was still up.

Epitaph

I wrote this so that I could speak to you,
hold your hand, give you the sensation
that I am with you,

when in all likelihood
you did not so much
as pass me on the street.

I wish we had been born
in the same part of the world, as neighbors,
ideally as members of the opposite sex
within a socially-acceptable age range
for courtship.

But I doubt any of that happened.

I suppose I should tell you:
I married a girl with beautiful eyes
and a fast mouth.
Those have always been my weaknesses.

She almost made me forget
I hadn't met you.

But in the end, I have to acknowledge
the infinitesimally small possibility

that you were even born in my lifetime.

That's why I chiseled these words
with the best diamond I could produce,
engraved this one poem
across every other,
tying them together, a wedding band for you,
scrawling in black
over my written portrait,
I will find you.

I know this is of little reassurance.
If my poems have made it out to you
and I am a famous poet,
then I am probably dead already.

You will have to marry a man
who distracts you from it.

But in your deep heart,
remember these last lines,
one vow I can still make.
If any of my words rang true,
if I helped you glimpse
for even a moment
the white fire that is inside of us,
believe this:

    the mere idea of you

gives me the strength

to live forever.

And somewhere,

in a tunnel of light

or a sea of darkness,

I will be waiting.

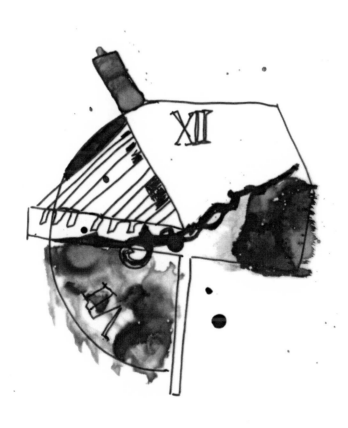

Love Story

for Jack Gilbert

When his herpes infection moved into his brain,
Clive Wearing, the brilliant pianist and conductor,
lost the ability to form new memories.
He was doomed to a perpetual present,
a purgatory of enlightenment documented in his journal:
8:31 AM: Now I am really, completely awake.
9:06 AM: Now I am perfectly, overwhelmingly awake.
9:34 AM: Now I am superlatively, actually awake.

Whenever his wife returns from the bathroom,
he falls to his knees, kisses her neck
because his last memory of her
is from decades ago.

In return, she takes him to the piano.
He doesn't know that he can play anymore –
doesn't remember her taking him there, day after day,
to practice.

But when she puts his hands on the keys,
his fingers start to move.
He lets his eyebrows peak painfully,
an exhausted man
allowed a moment of rest.

When the sonata is finished, he shakes uncontrollably.

None of the doctors know why.

Perhaps it's the shudder of losing again

what the music had given him – a sense of time.

The next day, he will be reunited with his wife,

smell her hair, feel her beloved hands

press his against the keys.

He will play *Lii-Presto Agitato*,

his desire blooming across the silence

of those many rich years.

Born Outside
the Horseshoe Cafe

Bellingham, we bummed so many cigarettes.

We tipped well because the waitresses were cute.
We joined noise bands
and learned how to play the downtown.
We drank away the last of our all-age venues.

The mountains reminded us of our parents.
Even more than God, we loved strangers.
Our hearts swung their fists of flame,
silly,
useless,
out of place,
talented,
tired,
uniform,
late for class.

We wore shirts designed after static.
We went mad inside, fell to our knees inside.

We kissed and wept, but most of the time,
we did these things inside

and then wrote poems about it.

We wore the sidewalks in circular wanderlust.
We repeated our parent's revolutionary slogans
without knowing it.

We stayed up past three a.m. and pretended
we did it more often.

We were in love with the clasp of the ocean.
We pressed applause to our ears like a shell.

We worshipped so many idols
looking only
for ourselves.

Stained Glass Birdsong

When I come to see her, my mother is often

on the porch, smoking and reading the Bible.

I stand in the window, filling with silence

as the light pours over me, wondering why psalms

never took to my lungs like cancer,

why I reject faith,

why I write and re-write the holy texts

in the color of my own strange language.

She inhales, turns a page so thin

it looks like shed skin,

like the shucked-off mortality of Christ

left behind as he went up his flaming ladder

to the Sistine sky.

BOOK THREE

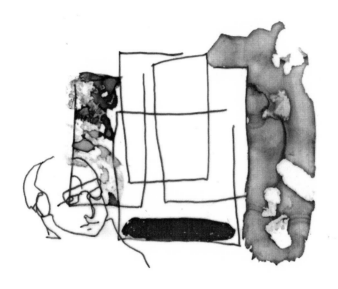

Desire

Some days I stand at the window looking out
over the parking lot and the trees beyond it,

trying to describe the gaping hole in my chest,
that rusty shed I call a heart in poetry
because I don't know any better word.

Then I daydream about the wilderness,
how the streams and mountains will take me,

how I will go out among them
looking for the holy texts,
the truth written in the soil, the rocks.

We were all born to love one thing.
I was born to love the heavy wilderness
as the light pours down across it,

filtering though the air alive
with the symphony of our ceaseless want.

Black Twine, Silver, Hallways

That night I slept in the cabin, the wind came over it like a black tongue.

Like the heart of a single mother that had been licked clean

until all it needed was God. Like a horse with its skin stripped,

with wide marble eyes and a black paintbrush that followed it.

That wind as warm as the scent of pine burning, the scent

of Dad's company picnics in the county where the men burned wood

in great barrels and laughed thickly under gray clouds heavy with soot.

Like a grandfather in the hours of his deepest wisdom,

the wind pressed my face against sleep and held it there, half-dreaming,

while one strand of thin moonlight worked only two things in the room

to life, made them into kites hung in the resin, inside the black of me,

where my chest dreamed suspended with two large birds

made of flattened silver, that night like a tomb that was a lullaby,

its skin and ink that was mixed with lead, halls of knowing

that the soul went on forever, like the wind pulling the hair of the night

over its eyes, when I slept in a cabin, when I was a boy

on some island, on some family vacation

I can no longer remember.

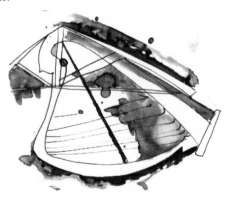

The Pineal Gland

Descartes called this structure *The Seat of the Soul.*

But we've since found it only regulates hormonal functions and sleep.

What a disappointment.

I wonder if part of the soul, at least, sits there.

Maybe we should call the Pineal Gland

The Seat of the Soul during High School.

Maybe the soul isn't shaped like a little king,

but like a spider web —

its throne elaborate, breathing,

its limbs like the bushes

in a garden maze.

The Simple Alphabet

Mark Rothko was a lonely man. He spent a lot of time drinking coffee and designing new ways to represent his least favorite shape, which was the square. Outside the bookstore, he stared at the sign. He stared at the doorway. He wondered, Why did it turn out that a human being's soul is in the shape of a square? Why this most boring shape? Why couldn't the human soul look like a sparkler at night in an aunt's driveway with the smoke of a barbeque hanging around it? But it looks like a square, after all. Not a star with icicles of glass breathing from its nitrogen eye, not the edge of a lake lapping gently against reeds in the fog, not a field at sunrise that opens like a pair of hands. A square. Maybe two or three squares. So he went to video stores and laundry mats more than museums, spent a lot of time staring at the sidewalk. *Well*, he thought, *at least it's a practical structure*, and made an alphabet of square. He made squares of insomnia and squares that looked like a father's shoulders. He made squares like sheets of music or trays of silverware. He made squares like his wife. He mostly made dark squares, squares like classy night clubs or strip joints after closing. But he also made squares like Tequila, squares that smash the eyes in like a windshield, and he made squares that were filled with wind from some deep canyon. That canyon is what the soul comes from, he must have thought, and marveled at its great and terrible size, the size that brought him to tears, then stood sighing and shaking his head outside the supermarket's sliding doors.

Stone Birdsong

When they open my mom on the autopsy table,

expecting cancer or pneumonia,

they'll find instead all the calcified years

of single motherhood inside her.

Statues of men will fill her

like a garden – all the men she loved

and the lives she could have had with them.

The birds that sit on the statues

will have voices like water moving over stone.

And a young lab technician,

against the advice of her colleagues,

will wander into that place,

never to be seen again.

The Funeral Parade

When a car passed my house a night,

its headlights lingering on my wall,

I'd imagine it was the deathglow of a stranger.

That an old woman wearing an apron

had clutched her chest and run outside,

feeling the call of the Almighty,

radiant at the opening seams of her body.

I'd watch the headlights for hours:

this one a businessman, this one a child too-soon,

this a mother nursing her infant

who will be bleached now, forever, albino.

Strangers lifted out of their skins, their torsos blooming

into arachnid streetlamps, all their secrets and sacred codes

returning to the heavens like a library fire.

When I saw Hiroshima on the television,

I didn't believe what my teachers told me about death.

I wrote in my stories that the blast had come

from one million hearts leaping out of their chests.

I believed the saxophones of our cities

when they wailed that no hunger is insignificant,

that every heartbeat is a stuttering step to return

to the white furnace that first forged us

out of rainwater and curling ribbons of acid,

that filled our veins with fire

and made them hiss against the stethoscope

like kerosene.

So when I saw your picture in the news today,

Dying Sudanese Man Eats Cow Dung,

I wanted to sit by my window

the way I used to as a boy,

to watch the headlights gleam off the feral dumpsters

until I knew that yours were passing,

until you beaconed beyond yourself,

a lantern sea of halogen doves,

your hopes flying back to God.

Our Scent of Iron and Mystery

Before we were animal, we were something else.

Ash in the bloodstream. Silk billowing in a red, wet room.

Like question marks we slid into the world,

this spacious vent of white air and traffic.

Life Skills

A Monologue

Once, after forgetting to take the garbage out, I received an important lecture from my mother about *life skills*. Since then, I've kept a detailed list of the abilities I master.

Greatest among these is the ability to come back from the dead.

I can also make ridiculous claims.

My pulse counts the proximity of lightning.

Mom used to yell at me for losing my coat at school. "What are you doing in that head of yours?" she'd ask. *Causing solar eclipses, mom.*

Solar eclipses.

I hang out with a lot of slam poets, so I've recently added a new ability to my list: I can compliment strangers in a way that confuses them.

You are what the Great Flood would look like if it had only swallowed the gardens outside of orphanages.

I've still got a lot of work to do if I want to flesh out my list. For example, I'm not yet comfortable around attractive women. I don't keep a day planner. I've never defeated anyone in a duel. My stance is not especially powerful. I do not sling amethyst rocks.

But I am at my desk with the candle burning. I am at the bookstore trying to buy faith. I'm in my classroom writing poetry while not paying attention in poetry class. These are my abilities.

I like to hang out with my friends because they have the ability to love things without naming them, and I want them to train me. At high altitude.

Maybe at a dojo.

We like to practice our skills while drinking beer and playing air hockey, wondering: if we were to sail all the way to heaven, would we get the bends all over again? Would there be candles lit inside our veins and the millions of abilities we contain begin writing books on the laced miracle of our inner skin?

When I was seven I learned how to hear a man breaking into my mother's ribcage at night. So in her name, I'm currently working on life skill number forty-four: feeling like a man even when you don't win something, or own something, or take something.

I'm not done yet. But I'm working on it.

And if my child named Someday ever forgets to take the garbage out, I'll take her aside and say, *You are the best broken machine this universe has ever ridden on. I hope you carry your faults until you wear them into grace.*

It doesn't matter how powerful your stance is, as long as you write music with the way life's fists touch your skin.

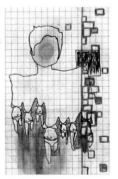

Enough

In India there are five year olds
who do arithmetic at calculator speeds
working for merchants in the marketplace.

What brilliant survival, death refuted
again and again from their abacus hearts.

And the greatest wonder isn't how they add
one thing to the next, but rather how they subtract
the days of noise and hunger, how they clean themselves,
the way we all have to, from the ghosts
of impatient strangers.

How do they make life sweet
and hurtful enough to be worth the trouble of surviving?
Do their thoughts rise to them
as elegant strings of numbers?

It's been one hundred and thirteen days
since my cousin went to look for work,
one tells her friend under the white moon.

I whispered to the rude, rich widow today
that when I subtract my current age
from my father's age of death, the difference
is how old my mother was when she died.

I breathed four more times today than usual.
That means I was half a percent more alive.

Maybe a teenage boy lies half-dreaming,
listening to the leaves of an almost bare tree,
counting each tick.
Each time a leaf turns, he decides,
a year passes.
When the wind picks up, decades whirl,
the rivers rise and fall in time-lapse,
seasons flash across the mountains
until time spirals even beyond his grasp
and he comes to the edge of counting,

where the tents of the market have scattered,
the rugs unraveled to their purple threads,
dust and mud had buried the coins
that someone will unearth in the vast, uncountable future
and hold like they were worth
all the hands that touched them.

He might stir then, his dream shifting as he remembers
a sister who passed away.
If we all inhale at precisely the same moment,
he tells the shoppers and vendors in the market,
and our breaths last four seconds,
the sky will change color

and my sister will come back from the river,

counting her steps to meet me.

Siberia

I want to be buried in Northern Siberia
among the ancient trees, the snow coming down
like my mother's hands.
The air baptismal in its lethal purity.

My kids will stand in fur-lined hoods.
They'll sprinkle my ashes across the white, saying
Here are the words
on his last page.

My sister will recount how I wrote this poem
one night in winter, drinking coffee.
How I'd never even been to Siberia.
How I'd probably just seen
some documentary about it.
How I'd only wanted to be laid to rest
far from the world's religions,
in a place close to God.

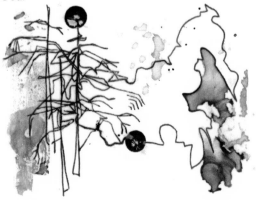

Maple Seeds

There was no gravestone for boyhood.
No service in the forest by my trailer park.
Someone should have sent wordless invitations,
filled our mailboxes with maple seeds – one to each man
who'd know their source.

We'd leave our roommates taking bong hits or studying,
drive past the dock we used to dive from in the summer
that sunk two inches underwater when our voices changed,
rediscover the trails behind tin houses,
brush cobwebs aside with a reverence we never used to,
gather in the treeless valley where only the fastest of us
had dared to linger during tag.

Jon would be there, who'd eaten cat food by the handful,
and his brother, who'd named his decks of Magic cards
like New Age albums. The older bully Greg would swagger up,
potbellied by now but still standing tall
for the sake of all our pride.

Smoldering below his red hair, Jake would arrive last –
who'd once admitted, on the verge of crying,
that he'd always loved Joker more than Batman.
Who'd biked away with his CD collection
when his trailer caught fire in '93
and was found by authorities

lockjawed and tearless

ten miles down North Shore Road

where his mother had died the year before.

Boyhood never had a gravestone,

not even for him.

But if we met again, we'd make one.

A log carved with Jake's pocket knife,

ringed with maple seeds.

We'd stand around it until the past

became too deep to see the bottom of,

until we sighed the way our fathers did

and heard, far below us, the soft slip of the dock

sinking finally away from light.

Oak and Sunlight Birdsong

When they cut me open,
they'll find whole novels I swallowed too fast
so I could go back to playing video games.
They'll find too many mirrors,
some filled with my face,
some with the reflections of strange birds,
most of them filled with the faces of girls
who have deep circles under their eyes.

Maybe because of my mother, overworked women
have always looked beautiful to me.

Inside the back bedroom of my spine,
they'll find a lopsided movie projector
replaying a game of tag in a trailer park.

In my skull they'll find a chair
by a sunlit window
and a bottle of spilt wine
pooling like a black eye.

They'll find a field beyond the window,
and a book left fluttering on the sill.

They'll never know if I left before finishing it,
or if I was just going back,
reading over all the parts in the story I loved.

In the Snow

After I take them home, I keep driving.
The world running through my hands like white rope.
The night like glass above it.

Only a moment ago, my sister's car had been so full
of voices, jokes, shivering bodies, laughter,
advice on how not to slide into this or that lamp post.
Ben's feet over the back seats, Sam's lazy worrying in my ear:
We're going to die. Death is imminent. We're going to crash.

And when we didn't, when I brought them safely home
across the frost, it was not really a triumph –
only one of those daily feats we all perform
as a matter of living. Jessica got out quietly, full of sleep,
Weston and Kim on either side of her.
Ben gangled from the trunk and slipped home along the sidewalk.
Sam barely seemed grateful to have survived.

Now the car gropes loose and blind beneath me.
A moving starscape slides into the white
across some amnesiac line, and I find my way,
slow and curling, through the thick sleep of blue
painted in slabs beside the snow,
wondering how we survived the ice ages at all
without dashboard heaters.
Furless and rotten-toothed. Giving birth
like violent red ribbons in the tundra.

If she lives long enough, an old Inuit will walk across the ice

until it detaches and carries her into the arms of the Atlantic.

She falls asleep in a drifting pyramid of powder,

hair barely visible at the peak, like a black root.

Sometimes when I look at my friends,

trying to make clever conversation, half of me

is sucked into the whirlpool of studying them:

What is it in there, I think, that made us want to do it –

to survive just long enough to cough out one more generation?

Jessica's face pink and sobbing in an igloo somewhere

while she heaves out another steaming child.

Sam harpooning a mammal the size of a village, balanced

in a small boat over gasping hypothermia. *We're going to die.*

Ben drawing on a cave wall about what has mattered most

for the vast and defining majority of our existence:

mammoths, seals, man-shaped evolutionary competitors with stones

and sharpened bone – the story of our lives,

when we hoarded fire like a secret God.

My heater is finally working,

and I wonder if this is what it was all for –

if our ancestors instinctively knew

that a life of comfort would someday be available,

even to a small number of us.

Or if there was something else, buried deep

under the snowfall that covers our tracks. That black root of hair

waving like an unsurrendered flag as the ice floe goes down.

That final walk to the horizon where snow bends and whirls
like phantom arms, waving us home toward hard-earned oblivion,
honorable rest. Maybe what kept us going is an odd sense of pride,
the simple demand – not to live, but to choose in what way
we will let death come.

Or perhaps it was, after all, just about life: standing
beside your healthy child at sunset, pointing to the burning
chipped-glass ocean – a mirror to the fierce, living,
liquid hearths inside of us that we've kept
going this long.

A truck turns onto the street, headlights trumpeting,
then detaches and drifts away.

Silence rises to cover me
and I carry it through the snow

until I arrive home to sleep – warm, fragile,
against the odds.

About the Poet

In 2004, while twenty years old, Ryler Dustin set aside his fourth unfinished novel after hearing poetry at a local open microphone. Since then, he has performed and taught poetry across the U.S., edited the literary magazine Jeopardy, and helped organize the legendary Lobster Manor Basement Poetry Series. He is a winner of the Sue C. Boynton Poetry Contest, the Bart Baxter Poetry Competition and the Jack McCarthy Invitational Poetry Slam.

He'd like to thank his friends at Bellingham, Washington's *Poetry Night*. They are the reason he is writing poetry. He would also like to thank their mothers – for engaging, platonic conversation, rich with wisdom and matronly care.

In August 2008, he began studying poetry at the University of Houston's MFA program.

Some Suggested Poetry
Li-Young Lee: *Rose*
David Ignatow: *Shadowing the Ground*
Jack Gilbert: *Refusing Heaven*
James Tate: *Return to the City of White Donkeys*
PoetryNight.org

Illustration Credits

OTHER GREAT WRITE BLOODY BOOKS

THE LAST AMERICAN VALENTINE: ILLUSTRATED POEMS TO SEDUCE AND DESTROY
24 authors, 12 illustrators team up for a collection of non-sappy love poetry
Edited by Derrick Brown

SOLOMON SPARROWS ELECTRIC WHALE REVIVAL
*by Buddy Wakefield, Anis Mojgani, Derrick Brown, Dan Leamen
& Mike McGee*

I LOVE YOU IS BACK
Poetry compilation (2004-2006)
by Derrick Brown

BORN IN THE YEAR OF THE BUTTERFLY KNIFE
Poetry anthology, 1994-2004
by Derrick Brown

DON'T SMELL THE FLOSS
New Short Fiction Pieces
by Matty Byloos

THE CONSTANT VELOCITY OF TRAINS
New Poetry
by Lea Deschenes

HEAVY LEAD BIRDSONG
New Poems
by Ryler Dustin

UNCONTROLLED EXPERIMENTS IN FREEDOM
New Poems
by Brian Ellis

LETTING MYSELF GO
Bizarre God Comedy & Wild Prose
by Buzzy Enniss

CITY OF INSOMNIA
New Poetry
by Victor Infante

JUNGLESCENE: UNDERGROUND DANCING IN LOS ANGELES
A sweaty modern photographic historical journey
by Danny Johnson

WHAT IT IS, WHAT IT IS
Graphic Art Prose Concept book
by Maust of Cold War Kids and author Paul Maziar

NO MORE POEMS ABOUT THE MOON
by Michael Roberts

LIVE FOR A LIVING
New Poetry compilation
by Buddy Wakefield

SOME THEY CAN'T CONTAIN
Classic Poetry compilation
by Buddy Wakefield

SCANDALABRA
(Winter 2008)
New poetry compilation
by Derrick Brown

ANIMAL BALLISTICS
(Winter 2008)
New Poetry compilation
by Sarah Morgan

COCK FIGHTERS, BULL RIDERS, AND OTHER SONS OF BITCHES
(Winter 2008)
An experimental photographic odyssey
by M. Wignall

THE WRONG MAN
(Winter 2009)
Graphic Novel
by Brandon Lyon & Derrick Brown

YOU BELONG EVERYWHERE
(Winter 2009)
A memoir and how to guide for travelling artists
by Derrick Brown with Joel Chmara, Buddy Wakefield, Marc Smith, Andrea Gibson, Sonya Renee, Anis Mojgani, Taylor Mali, Mike McGee & more.

writebloody.com